DEC 2010

Radio-Controlled CAR Experiments

More **Cool** Books

Science Projects with Technology

Electric Motor Experiments
ISBN-13: 978-0-7660-3306-1

Radio-Controlled Car Experiments
ISBN-13: 978-0-7660-3304-7

Robot Experiments
ISBN-13: 978-0-7660-3303-0

Solar Cell and Renewable Energy Experiments
ISBN-13: 978-0-7660-3305-4

Cool
Science Projects
with
Technology

Radio-Controlled
CAR
Experiments

Ed Sobey, PhD

To kids everywhere who pick up an R/C controller and
conduct experiments in science and technology

Acknowledgements

Thanks to Coyote Central for offering my classes in remote-controlled
cars and to the kids who signed up for them.

Copyright © 2011 by Ed Sobey

Library of Congress Cataloging-in-Publication Data

Sobey, Edwin J. C., 1948–
   Radio-controlled car experiments / Ed Sobey.
     p. cm. — (Cool science projects with technology)
   Includes bibliograph ical references and index.
   Summary: "Presents several science projects dealing with radio-controlled cars"—
Provided by publisher.
   ISBN 978-0-7660-3304-7
   1. Automobiles—Models—Radio control—Juvenile literature. 2. Science projects—
Juvenile literature. I. Title.
TL237.S63 2011
796.15'6078—dc22

                                           2009037896

Printed in the United States of America

092010 Lake Book Manufacturing, Inc., Melrose Park, IL

10 9 8 7 6 5 4 3 2 1

To Our Readers: We have done our best to make sure all Internet Addresses in this
book were active and appropriate when we went to press. However, the author and
the publisher have no control over and assume no liability for the material available
on those Internet sites or on other Web sites they may link to. Any comments or
suggestions can be sent by e-mail to comments@enslow.com or to the address on the
back cover.

♻ Enslow Publishers, Inc., is committed to printing our books on recycled paper. The
paper in every book contains 10% to 30% post-consumer waste (PCW). The cover board
on the outside of each book contains 100% PCW. Our goal is to do our part to help
young people and the environment too!

Photo Credits: Ed Sobey, except for US Patent and Trademark Office, p. 13;
Shutterstock, pp. 31, 44, 64, 83, 88; Stephen F. Delisle, p. 29.

Cover Photo: Cat London / iStockphoto.com (teen) and Shutterstock (car).

Contents

Experiments with a 🏅 symbol feature Ideas for a Science Fair Project.

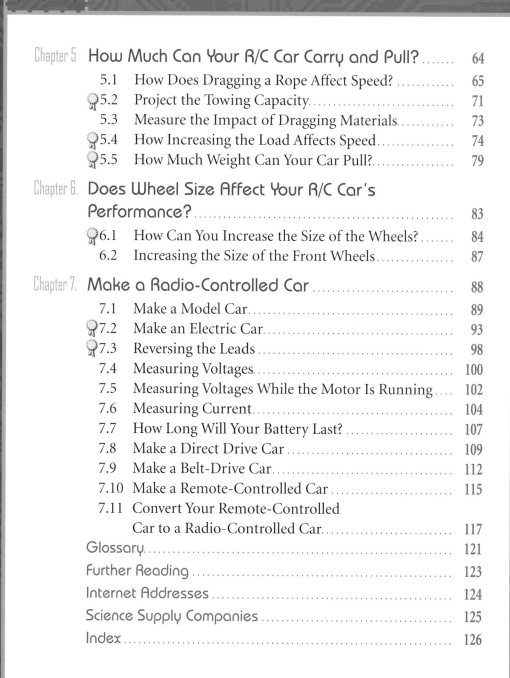

Experiments with a 🏅 symbol feature Ideas for a Science Fair Project.

Start Your Motors— An Introduction

When you walk past a radio-controlled (R/C) car, can you resist picking up the controller and driving it? For many people, R/C cars are almost impossible to pass up. They give you the ability to travel fast and to control motion far from your physical reach. You can zip the car up and down a sidewalk or through a house while standing in one spot.

Just by operating an R/C car, you are testing your reflexes and your ability to adjust your reactions as the car moves. Do you turn your body to align it with the car so that you know which way to steer? With practice you can learn how to control the car better—your brain adapts to each new position of the car. Can you steer it backward through a maze of books and boxes? Who can drive it fastest through a narrow racecourse? Can you control it in the next room without seeing where the car is?

An R/C car is a great tool for conducting experiments. You can test your own reflexes and abilities, along with the abilities of the car and its technology. From how far away can you control the car? How steep a hill can the car climb? Can it push another car out of the way? Figure 1 shows some examples of R/C cars.

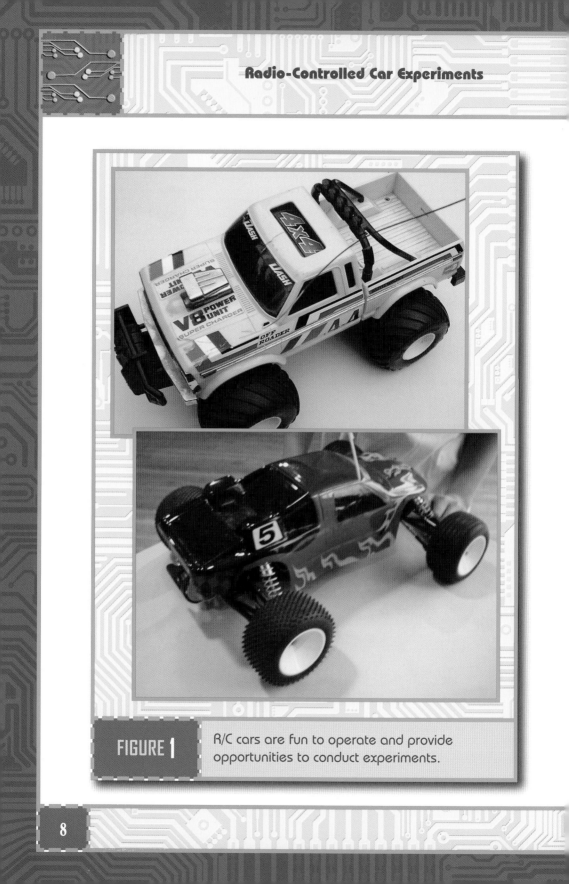

FIGURE 1

R/C cars are fun to operate and provide opportunities to conduct experiments.

The Scientific Method

If you like to play with technology and science, R/C cars offer a world of opportunities for conducting experiments. You can raise questions about how they operate, and then do experiments to confirm your ideas. Scientists do the same thing to make new discoveries. Not only do they learn new things, but they enjoy the process of learning through experimentation. This process is called the scientific method. It is a fun and natural way to make discoveries and learn. You ask questions, come up with possible answers, and devise experiments to see if your answers are right.

Conducting a scientific experiment includes making observations, measuring variables, collecting and analyzing data, researching scientific reports, and producing an attractive and easy-to-understand report. Simply making an R/C car isn't science.

Start your project by messing around with R/C cars. This is the best way to learn. Ask yourself questions about how they operate and what they can do. As you learn more, ask better and more detailed questions. Before running an experiment, think of a possible answer, or hypothesis. The experiment can test whether your hypothesis is correct.

A good question is one that you can answer by running a test and collecting data. Being able to represent that data in a graph helps people understand what you have discovered. As you conduct experiments, remember to change only one variable at a time. If you change more than one variable, you won't be able to tell which one caused the effects you see.

You could experiment with two or more car designs to see which works best. Or, you could use two different designs and compare how the car acts in each case. Once you start running your car, you can come up with many different experiments to try.

Be sure to use your new knowledge of R/C car technology as a way to conduct fun science experiments. Ask lots of questions. If you plan to enter a science fair, check the rules of the fair before getting too far along in your experiments.

Your first job is to get a notebook in which you can record information about each experiment you conduct. Each entry should have a date so that you can keep track of when you did each experiment. List the materials you use, and keep notes on what you try and what results you observe. Add sketches of designs and circuits that you use. Add photos if you can. You will be able to build on these notes for a long time.

Safety First

The projects included in this book are perfectly safe, but read these safety rules before you start any project.

1. Do any experiments or projects, whether from this book or of your own design, under the supervision of a science teacher or other knowledgeable adult.

2. Read all instructions carefully before proceeding with a project. If you have questions, check with your supervisor before going any further.

3. Maintain a serious attitude while conducting experiments. Fooling around can be dangerous to you and to others.

4. Wear approved safety goggles when you are working with a flame or doing anything that might cause injury to your eyes.

5. Have a first-aid kit nearby while you are experimenting.

6. Do not put your fingers or any object other than properly designed electrical connectors into electrical outlets.

7. Do not operater your R/C car in a thunderstorm.

8. Always wear safety goggles when working with chemicals or doing anything that might damage your eyes.

9. Do not eat or drink while experimenting.

10. Always wear shoes, not sandals, while experimenting.

The First Radio-Controlled (R/C) System

During the late nineteenth century, many inventors were working on a way to transmit signals without the use of wires. These inventors included Nikola Tesla, Guglielmo Marconi, David Hughes, Henrich Hertz, and others. The result was the invention of the wireless telegraph, or radio, by Nikola Tesla. In 1898, Tesla also invented a radio-controlled boat. Figure 2 shows a copy of part of his patent drawings of his invention.

In 1898, Tesla showed his model to the public at Madison Square Garden in New York City. He called his radio-controlled boat the teleautomaton. He believed that it would launch the era of radio-controlled robots. To make it work, Tesla invented a radio-controlled switch for operating the propeller, rudder, and lights. When the boat received a radio signal, it turned on one of the circuits. Using a series of mechanical parts, each of the desired functions (speed, direction, and lights) could be controlled with one switch.

It took sixty years before other technologies (transistors and plastics among others) were developed that allowed R/C toys to come to the marketplace.

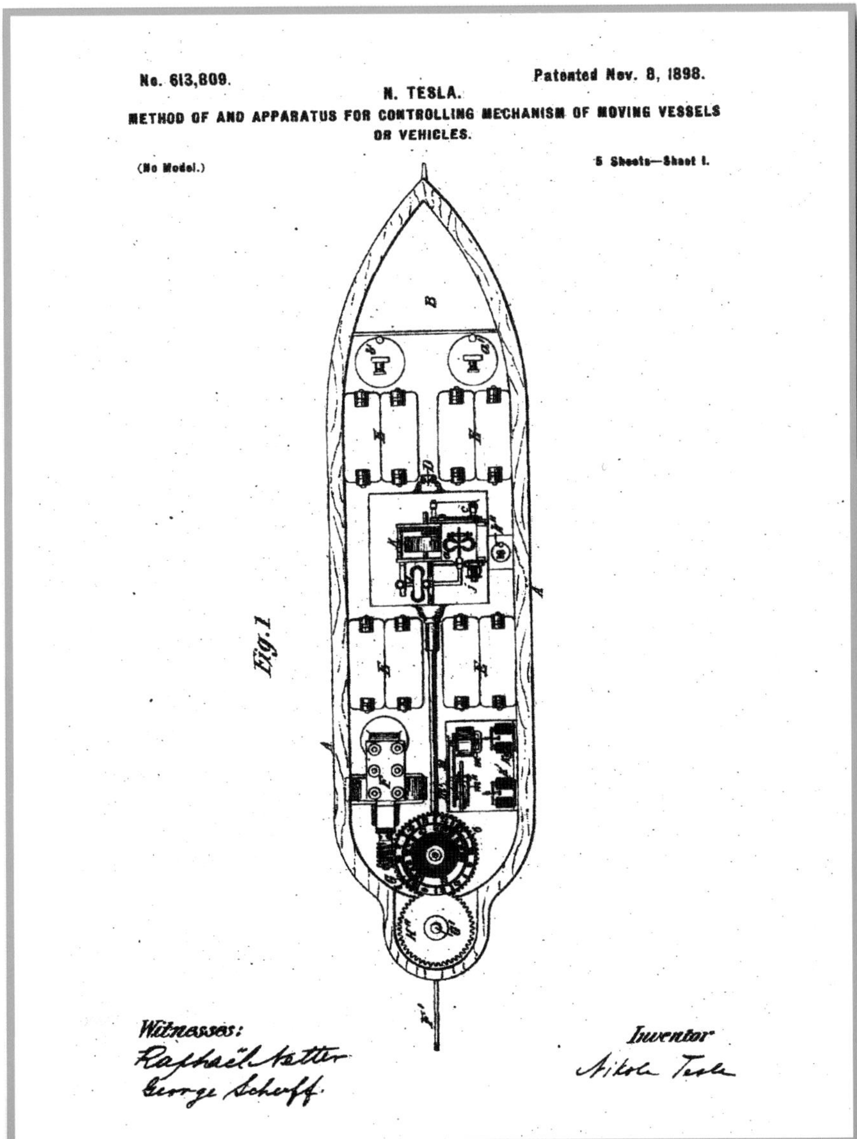

No. 613,809.

Patented Nov. 8, 1898.

N. TESLA.

METHOD OF AND APPARATUS FOR CONTROLLING MECHANISM OF MOVING VESSELS OR VEHICLES.

(No Model.)

5 Sheets—Sheet 1.

Fig. 1

Witnesses:

Raphael Netter
George Scherff.

Inventor

Nikola Tesla

FIGURE 2 The first radio-controlled device was a boat built by Nikola Tesla in the late nineteenth century.

Remote-Controlled Cars

Most people confuse remote control with radio control. Remote control affects behavior at a distance. Usually it involves sending electrical signals along wires between a control box and the car or other device being controlled. Turning on the hall light at home is an example of remote control. You do not turn a switch on the light fixture itself; instead you control the fixture from several feet away. When you turn the switch on, you let electricity flow to the lights.

Remote-controlled cars were common before radio-controlled toys. The battery-operated handheld controller usually had one or more switches. In its simplest form, a remote-controlled system works by allowing or interrupting the flow of electrical power to the car. Two wires carry electricity around a circuit.

How R/C Cars Work

Radio-controlled (R/C) cars can be powered by gasoline, electricity, or nitro. We will focus on the most common and least expensive type of motor: electric.

In electric R/C cars, both the car and the control unit carry several batteries. Typically, the car has a 9-volt transistor battery and four other batteries, usually AA. The 9-volt battery powers the electronic circuits in the car and the other batteries provide energy for the steering and drive motors. Inside the handheld controller is another 9-volt battery which powers the circuits and transmits the signal to the car.

Pressing the buttons or moving the controls closes switches inside the handheld unit. A circuit board interprets the pattern of the circuit the switches create. It generates and transmits a coded signal. The signal travels to the antenna of the handheld unit and is broadcast as a radio signal. Any cars operating at the same frequency (the number of times the signal changes per second) will receive this signal. They will execute the commands you send.

Inexpensive R/C cars operate at either 27 megahertz (MHz) or 49 MHz. These numbers represent the frequency of the radio signal that carries the coded message to the car. A 27-MHz signal cycles 27 million times each second. That sounds like a high-frequency signal, but your microwave oven operates much higher, at about 2.5 gigahertz (GHz), which is 100 times faster.

The car has an antenna to receive the radio signals. The antenna can either be visible or hidden inside the car. The radio signal received by the antenna goes to a circuit board, where the signal is decoded. Then power is sent to either of the two motors (steering or drive) in the desired direction (left or right; forward or backward).

Steering can be accomplished in several different ways. Most common methods use a small electric motor that rotates the front axle. R/C cars most often steer like an automobile: the front wheels are turned in the direction of desired travel. However, some models use a differential drive, like most mobile robots and army tanks. In this case each side of the car has its own drive motor and there is no steering motor. To turn the car, one motor is driven faster than the other.

There are many variations of this basic design. The best way to really understand how an R/C car works is to take one apart. You can do this by continuing with Experiment 1.1 and Experiment 1.2, where you will take apart an R/C car and a motor. This will help you become familiar with all the components of an R/C car. (The knowledge will also help you if you decide to make your own R/C car in Chapter 7.) However, if you already have a functioning R/C car and prefer to get started with it right away, you can go to Chapter 2.

Take Apart an R/C Car

COOL!

Do not take apart your favorite operating R/C car. Find one that is not working. You may be able to buy one from a garage sale or thrift store for only $1 (see Figure 3).

1. Check to see if the car works. If it does, you might not want to take it apart. Instead, find another, nonworking car.

2. Start by taking apart the controller. Although the R/C car might not respond to the controller, the controller might still work. First test the controller with another R/C car that uses the same frequency. (The frequency is written on both controllers and cars.) Try replacing the old batteries with new ones if they do not work at first.

3. Often one or two screws hold the front and rear halves of

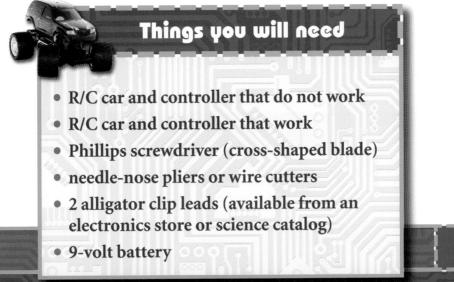

Things you will need

- R/C car and controller that do not work
- R/C car and controller that work
- Phillips screwdriver (cross-shaped blade)
- needle-nose pliers or wire cutters
- 2 alligator clip leads (available from an electronics store or science catalog)
- 9-volt battery

FIGURE **3** | Students take apart R/C cars purchased at a thrift store. Even if the cars don't work, many of the parts may be usable.

the plastic controller together. Remove these and open the case (see Figure 4). As you do, the antenna will likely fall out. It is connected by wire and is usually held in place by a screw. You can remove this screw to take out the antenna, or cut the wire with wire cutters.

Look at the switches on the circuit board. How do they transform your finger movements into switching on and off electric current? How many different kinds of switches can you find? Do not throw these away, as you may find uses for them in later experiments and model building.

4. Now start on the car. Flip it over to search for screws, holding the car body to the frame. Remove the screws and keep them in a cup or plate. You may have to remove other parts to get a look at the motors and circuit board.

5. Check out the drive motor. Most drive motors are mounted above the left rear wheel (see Figure 5).

6. Locate the motor shaft. In Figure 5, the shaft has a small golden gear on it. The small gear meshes with another gear in a gearbox. Count the number of gears and note

switch

circuit board

FIGURE 4   Inside the hand-held controller are switches and a circuit board.

their sizes. The small gear on the motor shaft drives a larger gear in the gearbox. That large gear is probably on an axle with a smaller gear that meshes with another large gear. When small motorized gears mesh with larger gears, the larger gears slow the rotation of the motor.

Why would you want to slow the speed of rotation? Since the motor spins so fast, it is not powerful enough to drive the car. If the motor were connected directly to the wheels, it would not have enough spinning power to accelerate the car. Gears reduce the speed but increase the spinning power, or torque. For the same energy output

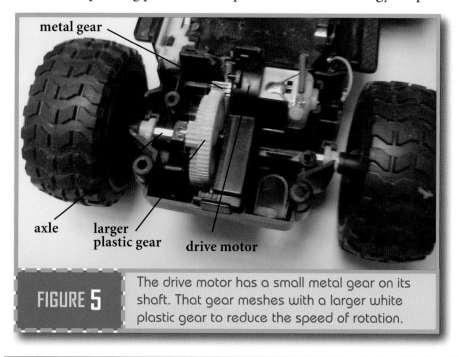

metal gear

axle   larger
       plastic gear   drive motor

FIGURE 5   The drive motor has a small metal gear on its shaft. That gear meshes with a larger white plastic gear to reduce the speed of rotation.

from the motor, you can have either more power or speed, but not both.

7. Look for a differential (a series of gears) in the middle of the drive axle that connects the two drive wheels. Differentials allow one wheel to spin faster than the other as the car turns. Without one, the tires wear too much (due to friction) as the inside wheel skids along the ground. On R/C cars this is not a big problem, as you will never get a flat tire, but in real cars and trucks it is a problem. If your model has a differential, open it up and figure out how it works.

8. You can test the drive motor to see if it works. Clip an alligator clip lead to each motor terminal and connect the two leads to a 9-volt battery for just a second. If the motor spins, you just found a useful part. You can either remove the motor and use it elsewhere, or try to get this model operating again.

9. Next look at the steering (see Figure 6). Turn the front wheels left and right. Do you see something move in a gearbox and motor? How does the motor deliver power to turn the wheels? To see if the steering motor works, connect it briefly to a 9-volt battery using the alligator clip

leads. If it does work, you can either extract it or keep it connected to the steering mechanism.

10. If both motors work but the car does not, check out the power switch. (The power switch is usually on the bottom or back of the car.) To test it, use alligator clip leads to connect the switch in series with a battery and motor. Switches are often the parts that fail first in any toy or appliance. If the switch is the only thing wrong with the car, you can either replace the switch or bypass it with wire.

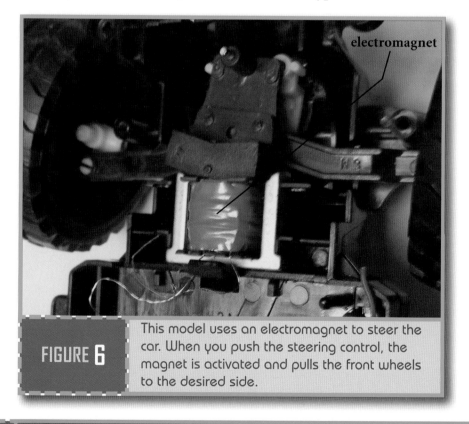

electromagnet

FIGURE 6

This model uses an electromagnet to steer the car. When you push the steering control, the magnet is activated and pulls the front wheels to the desired side.

11. Consider taking the wheels off the axles. Usually the wheels fit snugly on the axles. You can remove them by gently pulling, as they are probably held by friction or glue. However, you may find them more useful if you leave them on the axles.

12. Does the car have electric lights? Do they work when connected to a battery? Can you extract them and use them in another project? Is there anything else to explore?

   Keep looking for discarded R/C cars to take apart. Each one is likely to use different designs, and you can learn from them all.

   What else can you do with the R/C car you took apart? Even if it was broken before you took it apart, you can use its components. If the two motors work, take them out. Cut the wires that supply them with electric power, but leave enough to be able to connect them to a new power supply. Gears, wheels, and switches may be useful in other projects. If the radio-control system works, take out the circuit board and try connecting the wires to small lights or buzzers using alligator clip leads. You may be able to use the radio control system to build something new. If either of the two motors does not work, you can take one apart in the next experiment.

Take Apart a Motor

1. Before taking a nonworking motor apart, notice whether it attracts small metal objects such as screws. If it does, the motor has magnets inside.

2. Hold the motor by its shaft and look at the opposite end. Almost all R/C car motors look the same. Use a small flat screwdriver to pry up the two small metal tabs that hold the white plastic piece tight against the metal cylinder (see Figure 7).

3. Once they are pried upward, you can push on the motor shaft to get the parts out. The plastic end cap has two metal bars (copper conductors) that act like springs.

Things you will need

- nonworking motor from an R/C car
- small flat screwdriver
- small metal objects, such as screws
- 2 alligator clip leads
- 9-volt battery

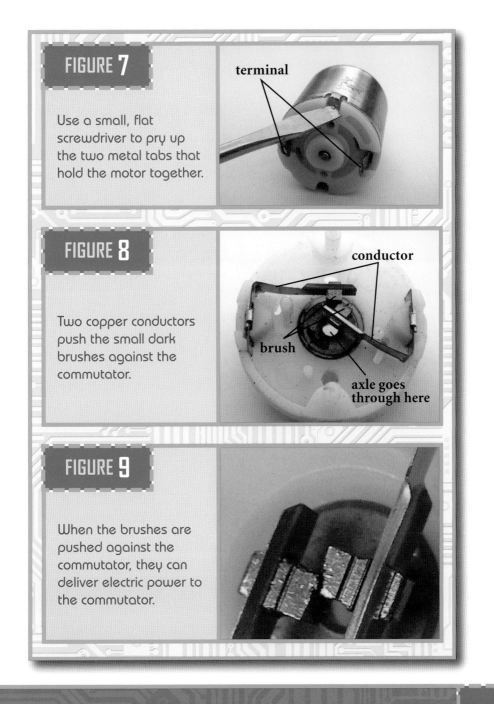

FIGURE 7

Use a small, flat screwdriver to pry up the two metal tabs that hold the motor together.

terminal

FIGURE 8

Two copper conductors push the small dark brushes against the commutator.

conductor

brush

axle goes through here

FIGURE 9

When the brushes are pushed against the commutator, they can deliver electric power to the commutator.

They push against the axle (see Figure 8). Look closely at the ends of these metal bars. They each have a small piece of dark material called a brush (see Figure 9). The brush makes contact with the commutator, which conducts electricity to the motor. Follow the metal bars in the other direction to see where they connect outside the motor. Their ends, opposite from the ends with brushes, are the motor terminals where you clip the battery lead wires (see Figure 10). Electricity passes from one battery terminal to the connected motor terminal, then through the metal conductor and brush to the axle. It returns to the battery through the other brush, conductor, and motor terminal.

4. Inside the motor case are two magnets. If you want, push the end of the screwdriver between the magnets and the case to pry them out.

5. The part that spins, including the axle or motor shaft, is the rotor (see Figure 11). Look at the commutator, the area of the axle where the brushes contact it (see Figure 12). You will see dark marks where the brushes have rubbed it. As the rotor turns, different parts of the rotor contact the brushes and receive electric current. This is the magic of simple motors. As the motor spins, the

FIGURE 10 Two terminals carry electrical power to and from the motor. The electromagnets are mounted on the rotor, which is on the motor shaft. Two permanent magnets are inside the motor case (above the rotor).

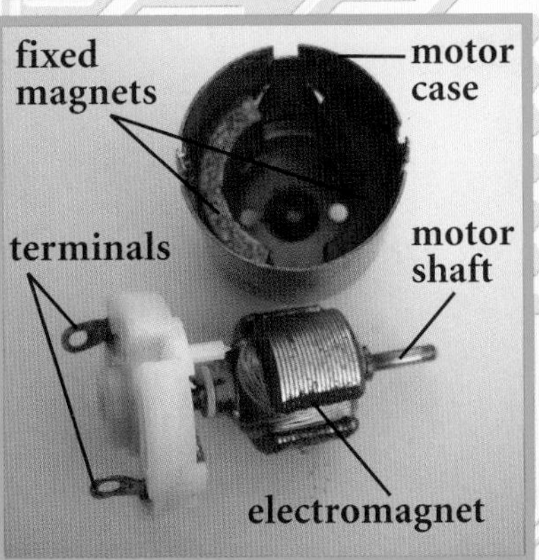

fixed magnets
motor case
terminals
motor shaft
electromagnet

FIGURE 11

The rotor inside a motor has three electromagnets that are attracted to and repelled by fixed permanent magnets.

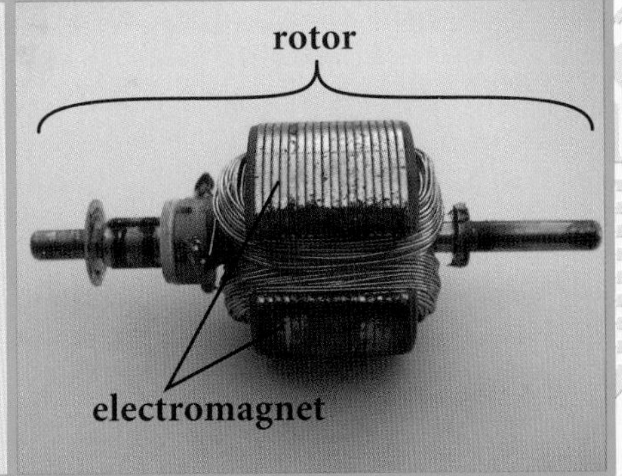

rotor
electromagnet

FIGURE 12

The commutator is on the motor shaft near the wire windings. It shows two dark rings where the brushes have rubbed against it.

copper wire
commutator

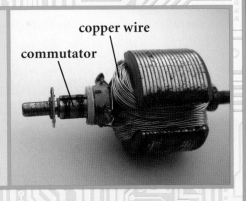

current is delivered to one of the three windings of copper wire. The current traveling through a winding creates an electromagnet. The electromagnet pushes and pulls against the two permanent magnets mounted in the motor case (Figure 10). As a winding gets close to one of the permanent magnets, the brushes lose contact with that winding but connect to the next winding. Now this next winding is pulled toward a permanent magnet. By constantly changing which winding receives electricity, the rotor is always pulled toward a magnet, and it continues to spin as long as electrical power is supplied.

6. Now try to get the motor back together. Getting the two permanent magnets back inside will be a bit tricky, and getting the brushes aligned with the commutator will be more difficult. But with perseverance, you can get it together. Then test the motor by connecting it to a battery. If it was not working before, you may have fixed whatever the problem was and may now have a working motor. Sometimes rust forms in motors or dirt gets into them. Simply taking a motor apart and twisting the motor shaft can get the rotor spinning again. If this happened, congratulations on your repair!

Electricity

The experiments and models in this book use electricity from batteries. Electricity is the flow of electrons, which are small negatively charged particles. It is measured by the force it exerts (voltage) and the size of the flow (current). Electricity is generated inside batteries through chemical reactions. Different types of batteries use different chemicals and reactions.

Each type of battery is capable of producing a maximum voltage, which is indicated on the battery. When connected to a motor, a battery causes electrons to flow through the wires to the motor and back to the battery. A battery and motor form a complete circuit when one wire connects

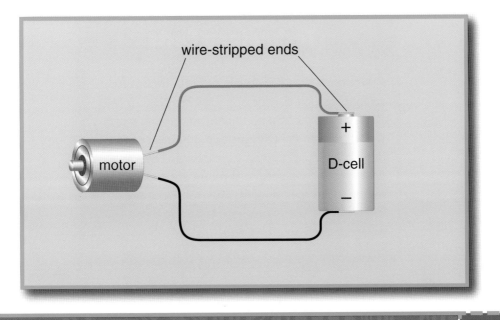

one side of the battery to one terminal on the motor, and a second wire connects the other side of the battery to the other terminal on the motor. Electrons can flow only when both connections are made.

In a circuit, the easier it is for the battery to cause electrons to flow, the larger the current it will produce. Adding resistance to the circuit reduces the current. An example of adding resistance is using wires that have become rusty. Even with the battery working at its top voltage, if rusty wires impede the flow of electrons, fewer electrons will reach the motor.

Technology Facts

How dangerous is a 9-volt battery? Not very, as long as you do not open the six battery cells that are inside. You can hold the terminals of a 9-volt battery on a finger and you will not feel the electricity. If you wet your finger with saliva and hold the battery to the wet spot, you might feel a mild tingling, but nothing more. Nine-volt batteries are safe to use in these experiments.

CHAPTER 2

How Fast Does Your R/C Car Go?

An R/C car is fast-accelerating, high-speed fun. But how fast are R/C cars? Let's find out. For these experiments, it's fine to use an inexpensive R/C car. You can find these at general merchandise stores and toy stores. You may be able to find one at a rummage sale or thrift store. Maybe your friend has an old car and would like to experiment with you. Hobby stores and online stores generally carry more expensive models. These, too, will work for the following experiments, but it is not necessary to spend a lot of money for these tests.

Calculate the Speed of Your R/C Car

Speed can be difficult to measure directly, so instead you will measure how long it takes a car to travel a known distance. (see Figure 13). The distance you choose will affect the calculated speed. On a course that is only 1 meter (3 feet) long, the car could still be accelerating before it reaches the end. On a much longer course, such as 7 meters (23 feet), the car will cover most of the distance at its top speed, and will thus have a higher calculated speed.

If you will use this experiment for a school science project, check to see what system of units they require (most likely,

Things you will need

- working R/C car
- low-friction floor or paved surface, such as a tennis court
- masking tape
- measuring tape or meterstick
- stopwatch
- notebook and pen
- a friend

FIGURE 13 To measure speed, lay out a straight test track to guide steering.

meters). Measure and record your distance measurement in the required system.

1. Pick a low-friction surface to use, such as a wood floor (not a deep carpet) or paved tennis court.

2. Mark a start line and stop line with masking tape. The course should be 3 to 6 meters (10 to 20 feet) long.

3. Measure the distance between the start and stop lines.

4. Have a friend use a stopwatch to measure the time as you run the car from the start to the finish line. Do the experiment at least three times and compare the time measurements.

5. Do the three measurements closely agree? If one is wildly different from the other two, repeat the experiment. If all three are very different see if you can understand why you are getting such different measurements. For example, if one measurement was twice as long as another, you would suspect that something was wrong. It should not take the car twice as long to travel the same distance unless conditions changed. Eliminate or change whatever is causing the differences.

6. When you can get three or more reliable measurements, average them. To do so, add the measurements and divide

by the number of trials you took. The average time should be close to your actual measurements.

7. Record the average speed of your car in your notebook. Note the units.

8. Compare the speed you calculated to one you are more familiar with. Convert your speed into miles per hour so that you can compare the speed of your R/C car with speeds of a car or bike. If you are converting from feet/second, remember there are 5,280 feet/mile, and 3,600 seconds per hour. If you are converting from meters/second, know that there are 1,609 meters/mile.

If your R/C car covers 6 meters in 3 seconds, its average speed is 2 meters per second, because 6 meters divided by 3 seconds equals 2 meters per second. To convert meters per second into kilometers per hour, multiply by 3,600 then divide by 1,000:

$$2\,\frac{\text{meters}}{\text{second}} \times 3{,}600\,\frac{\text{seconds}}{\text{hour}} \div 1{,}000\,\frac{\text{meters}}{\text{kilometer}} = 7.2\,\frac{\text{kilometers}}{\text{hour}}$$

How does your R/C car's speed of 7.2 kilometers per hour compare to speeds of cars and bikes?

Measuring Top Speed

In Experiment 2.1, your car started from a stop, and it took some time for it to reach top speed. The car started at zero velocity, so over the first second or two, it was not traveling at its maximum speed. If you waited for the car to get to top speed before timing it, would it average a higher speed over the test track?

In this experiment, you will start the car behind the start line. This will allow the car to reach its maximum speed before you start measuring time.

1. Start by estimating how far your R/C car needs to go to get to top speed. Watch the car while your friend starts it

Things you will need

- R/C car
- stopwatch
- masking tape
- a measured course (from Experiment 2.1)
- notebook and pen
- a friend

from a complete stop. From your observations, how far does it need to go? It may be about 1 meter (3 feet).

2. Whatever distance you think is correct, measure that far back from the start line and make another line with masking tape. This is the new start line; however, the timer will not start the watch until the car crosses the old start line. You want the car to accelerate to top speed before starting the timer.

3. Try several runs so the driver and timer are both working together. Then average the measurement from three or more trials and calculate the speed. Record all the data in your notebook.

Were the runs faster in this experiment? Were the individual time measurements as closely spaced as in the earlier experiment?

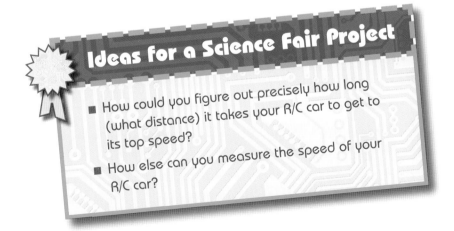

Ideas for a Science Fair Project

■ How could you figure out precisely how long (what distance) it takes your R/C car to get to its top speed?

■ How else can you measure the speed of your R/C car?

Measuring Speed with a Radar Gun

Measuring the speed of cars is typically done in one of three ways. The car's speedometer counts the number of rotations that the driveshaft makes. As the engine spins faster, the shaft spins faster, and either a mechanical or electrical device carries that information to the dashboard, where it is displayed. Car speeds can also be measured by radar guns. Police use radar guns to check for speeders. The gun sends out a pulse of radar (newer models use laser light instead of radar), and a receiver records the signal reflected by the car. By comparing the outgoing signal to the reflected signal, the gun can calculate the car's speed. GPS or global positioning systems calculate speed by marking the position of the car at two

Things you will need

- R/C car
- masking tape
- measuring tape
- low-friction floor or paved surface, such as a tennis court
- toy radar gun
- a friend to operate the radar gun
- notebook and pen

FIGURE 14

You can use a toy radar gun to measure your car's speed. You can also time cars over a set distance to calculate speed, then compare that to the speed recorded by a radar gun.

places and dividing the distance the car traveled by the time between the two measurements. You could also estimate your speed by timing how quickly you pass highway mile markers.

One way to measure the speed of a car is to use a radar gun. Toy radar guns (Figure 14) are available from Mattel® Hot Wheels® in stores or online. They are designed to be used with Hot Wheels® vehicles, so they will work well with your R/C car.

Use a radar gun to measure your car's top speed and compare that to the speed you calculated in Experiment 2.2. For the radar gun to get an accurate measure of your car's speed, you will need to drive the car along a straight line for several seconds.

1. On a smooth surface, such as a wood floor or paved tennis court, create a straight line of masking tape that is at least 6 meters (20 feet) long. Practice driving the car along this line at top speed.

2. When you are good at driving along the line, have a friend stand a few feet beyond the end of the line while holding the radar gun. Drive the car directly at your friend—without running it into him—and have him or her record the speed. It may take several attempts to get consistent results. Record the speeds in your notebook, and convert them into the units you used in the previous trials.

3. Compare the speed measured by the radar gun to the timed speeds from Experiment 2.2. Of the two sets of measurements, which do you think is more accurate? Why do you think one is more accurate? Is the radar gun or stopwatch easier to use? Can you improve the accuracy of either measurement?

Speed vs. Acceleration

In the previous experiments, we have dealt with speed. Acceleration is different from speed. Acceleration is how quickly something changes speed. Sitting at a stoplight, an automobile's speed and acceleration are both zero. When the car starts to move, its acceleration is large as it changes speed from zero to higher speeds. After reaching maximum speed, the driver eases off the accelerator and the car maintains a steady speed. Although the car is traveling at a high speed, that speed is not changing. The acceleration is close to zero. Letting the car coast to a stop causes the speed to decrease; it is decelerating (de-accelerating). Hitting the brakes makes it decelerate even faster. Eventually, the car is standing still and both speed and deceleration drop to zero.

In races, both speed and acceleration are important. Racing R/C cars over short distances favors a car with fast acceleration. Racing over long distances favors a car with high speed. In a long race, the time spent reaching full speed is a fraction of the total race time, so acceleration might not matter.

As you experiment with R/C cars, you see that they quickly accelerate to top speed. Directly measuring the rate of acceleration would be difficult because the distance required to go from standing still to operating at top speed is quite small. However, we can measure how quickly an R/C car decelerates.

41

Measuring Deceleration

If you have not estimated your R/C car's top speed, do that now. Follow the guidelines in Experiment 2.2 or 2.3 for measuring the speed either by timing the car over a set distance or with a radar gun. If you are timing the car, make sure that it has fully accelerated before you start the stopwatch. That is, let the car achieve top speed before it reaches the area you are using to measure the speed. Make sure that the road surface you use to measure top speed is the same as the one you will use in this experiment.

1. Use a piece of masking tape to mark a line on the ground.

2. Drive an R/C car at top speed until it crosses the line on the ground.

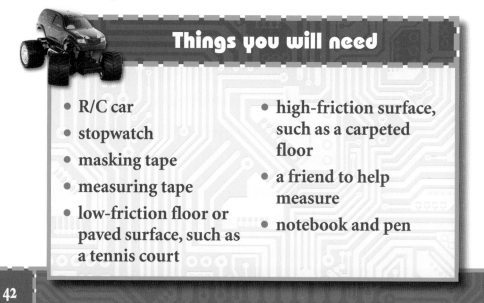

Things you will need

- R/C car
- stopwatch
- masking tape
- measuring tape
- low-friction floor or paved surface, such as a tennis court
- high-friction surface, such as a carpeted floor
- a friend to help measure
- notebook and pen

3. As the car crosses the line, release your hold on the remote control button so that the car begins to coast. At the same time, have your friend start the stopwatch.

4. When the car comes to a complete stop, have your friend stop the watch and record the elapsed time.

5. Repeat these steps several times to ensure that you are getting consistent results.

6. Divide the top speed (from Experiment 2.2 or 2.3) by the time it takes the car to come to rest. This is an estimate of the car's deceleration. It is a measure of how quickly the car goes from full speed to stop. Record this estimate for deceleration. Note that the units will be velocity/time. For example, if you measured speed in feet per second, deceleration would be feet per second per second, or feet per second squared.

7. Repeat the experiment on a floor surface with more friction, such as a thick carpet. You will need to measure the car's top speed on the new surface before estimating its deceleration.

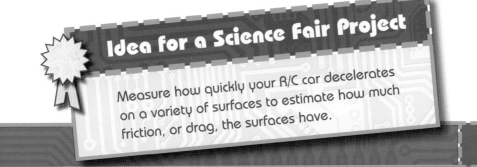

Idea for a Science Fair Project

Measure how quickly your R/C car decelerates on a variety of surfaces to estimate how much friction, or drag, the surfaces have.

What Is the Range of the Radio Control?

R/C cars are regulated by the Federal Communications Commission (FCC). This government agency oversees all electromagnetic emissions, including radio. It assigns frequencies according to how each type of radio device will be used, and licenses people and organizations to operate within their authorized frequencies. If you look at the small label affixed to your car and handheld controller, you will see information about the frequency the car uses and regulations about the use issued by the FCC. For R/C car operation, you do not need a license, but the signals are restricted to a very short range so that they will not interfere with other radios.

What Happens When the Car Goes Beyond Its Radio Range?

What is the radio range of your R/C car? What happens if you try to operate your R/C car beyond this range?

To conduct these experiments, you want to be in a safe environment, not a public street. You need to operate the car without the possibility of losing it or damaging it. A large paved playground or basketball court are good locations.

1. Drive your car along a straight path away from you. See how far it can travel.

2. Record this distance in your notebook. Also note what the car does at the end of its range.

What do you think might affect this distance? Weather conditions? The condition of your batteries? Other operating radios nearby? See if you can figure out what might change

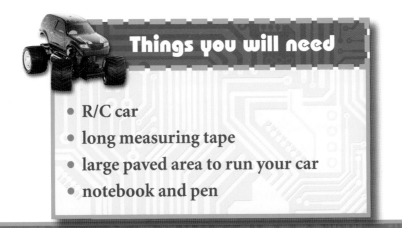

Things you will need

- R/C car
- long measuring tape
- large paved area to run your car
- notebook and pen

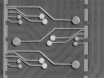

the range and do some experiments to check your ideas. For example, repeat this experiment under different weather conditions. Try when the weather is cold and when it is hot, or when it is dry and when it is raining. (**WARNING**: Do NOT operate your R/C car in a thunderstorm.)

How Well Do Radio Waves Travel in a Building?

Do radio waves easily penetrate walls of a building? Can you operate your car from a position several rooms away?

1. Operate the car in the same room you're in just to ensure that it is working properly. Drive the car forward.

2. Then move to an adjacent room and have a partner stay in the room with the car. Try operating it again, driving it forward. Your partner can tell you whether it receives the radio signals. Keep track of the result in your notebook.

3. Go farther away with more walls or other obstacles between transmitter and receiver. Can you find different types of walls to test? If you are inside a building and the car is outside, the radio waves would have a thicker wall to

Things you will need

-   R/C car
-   long measuring tape
-   large room with adjacent rooms
-   notebook and pen

penetrate. Can you estimate your car's radio range when different types of walls are between you and the car?

4. Compare the radio range while operating or without walls blocking the signal to the range while operating inside with partitions or walls. How much do the walls reduce the distance?

How Well Do Radio Waves Travel Through Other Materials?

COOL!

If you completely cover the transmitter with a blanket or pillow, can it still send signals that the car is able to receive? What other materials can you use to test the penetrating power of radio waves?

1. Wrap a towel around the transmitting antenna of the handheld controller. Then operate your R/C car to determine its range. Record your observations in your notebook.

2. Try surrounding the antenna with a mailing tube or a piece of plastic pipe. Measure the range of your car and record it.

3. Try other materials to see which ones reduce the range.

Things you will need

- **R/C car**
- **measuring tape**
- **variety of materials that might block the radio transmission: towel, cardboard tube, plastic tube, etc.**
- **large paved area or a large room**
- **notebook and pen**

Can You Control an R/C Car From Inside Your Car?

A car has a steel frame and body. How do they affect radio waves?

1. Place an R/C car on the ground near an automobile. With a parent's permission, try operating your R/C car while you are inside the automobile with the windows rolled up and the doors closed.

2. If you can operate the R/C car, what is the range? How does being inside a steel shell affect the radio waves?

3. If you have a portable radio, try operating the portable radio while sitting inside the car. Does it receive signals? Why or why not? Try both the AM and FM bands. Is there a difference?

Things you will need

-   **R/C car**
-   **automobile**
-   **measuring tape**
-   **portable radio**

Radio Range of an R/C Car and Antenna Lengths

The antenna on your handheld controller may extend. To fit the controller inside the packaging, manufacturers make the antenna collapse like a telescope. Have you tried operating your R/C car when the antenna is not fully extended? What do you think will happen?

1. With the transmitter antenna in its shortest position (the least amount of antenna exposed), find the operating range for the car. Record this distance, and measure the length of the antenna.

2. Extend the antenna 5 cm (2 in) and test the operating range. Did it change? Keep extending the antenna length by 5 cm. Hold the transmitter in the same position during each test. How far are you able to control the car? Record the data in your notebook.

Things you will need

- R/C car
- **long tape measure**
- **notebook and pencil**
- **graph paper**

3. Draw a graph using this set of data—measurement of antenna lengths and operating distance. Lay out a piece of graph paper with the horizontal axis showing the length of the antenna and the vertical axis showing the operating range (see below). Label the axes (Antenna Length and Operating Range) and show the units (inches and feet, or centimeters and meters). Graph the data using the graph paper. Lightly pencil a line between the data points.

4. Looking at the graph, what story does it tell? As the antenna is lengthened, what happens to the operating range? Is the line you drew straight? If so, it suggests that the same change in antenna length always causes the same extension in operating range. If the line bends, it means that the operating range increases at a different rate than the antenna length. Are there any other stories the graph can tell?

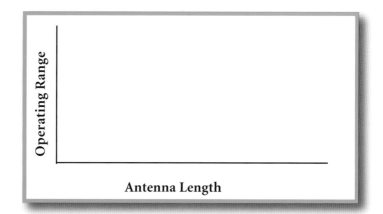

Lengthening the Antenna

Would extending the transmitter antenna farther increase the operating range? How could you find out?

An easy way to increase the length of the antenna is to attach one or more alligator clip leads.

1. Clip one lead onto the antenna (see Figure 15). What impact does it have on the range?

2. Try clipping a second lead onto the end of the first lead. Does that cause an additional increase in range?

3. Try shortening the antenna by pushing it to its most compact position on the handheld controller. Now test the impact of adding one or more clip leads.

If you do not have clip leads, try pieces of wire about 3 cm (12 in) long. Wrap one end around the antenna and

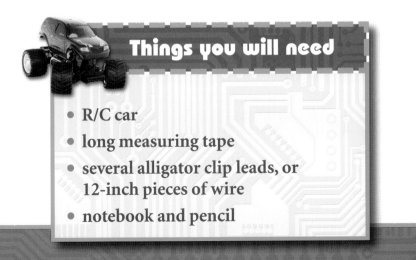

Things you will need

- R/C car
- long measuring tape
- several alligator clip leads, or 12-inch pieces of wire
- notebook and pencil

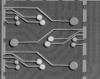

FIGURE 15 — You can extend the effective length of the antenna by clipping a wire to it.

let it hang down while you operate the car and test its range. Add more lengths of wire to see what impact they have.

What is the maximum range of your car? Is there a point where adding more clip leads or more wire does not increase the range? If so, what is the total length of this antenna/wire combination? Is it much greater than the fully extended metal antenna?

Compare the Length of the Antennas on the Car and Transmitter

How long is the antenna on the R/C car? To measure the car antenna, you will have to remove the car body because part of the antenna is inside the car.

1. Using a Phillips screwdriver, remove the screws that hold the R/C body to the frame. Find the antenna, a long piece of wire.

2. Measure the antenna from its extreme upper end to the point where it attaches (usually with a screw) to the car frame. It will be difficult to measure this precisely as the antenna is bent to fit through the opening in the car body. If you have a fabric tape measure handy, use that. If not, use a piece of string and lay it alongside the antenna. Pull the string taut as you slide your fingers down the

Things you will need

- R/C car
- meterstick
- fabric tape measure or piece of string
- Phillips screwdriver

antenna. Mark the length of the antenna on the string, and measure the string with a meterstick.

3. Once you have measured the antenna length, reassemble the car.

4. Now measure the length of the antenna on the handheld controller. Use the fully extended position. How closely do the two antenna lengths match? If they are approximately the same length, why do you think this is so?

Antennas are made to receive radio waves of particular wavelengths. The antennas on cell phones are much smaller than those on R/C cars because the radio waves they receive are much smaller. The antenna in the R/C transmitter and receiver should be the same length.

Does the Shape of the Receiving Antenna Matter?

Does the shape of the antenna affect the range? You cannot easily change the shape of the transmitter antenna, but the receiving antenna on the car can be bent into a loop. Let's try it.

Normally the receiving antenna is a lightweight wire that projects vertically from the car. What happens to the operating range if you coil this antenna into a circle?

1. Use a Phillips screwdriver to take the car body off the frame. Locate the antenna.

2. Coil the antenna and use a piece of masking tape to hold the wire in place. If the antenna is flexible enough, try two different diameter coils to see if that makes a difference. Measure the diameter of the coils and record it along with the operating distance. Does the operating range change when the wire is coiled from when it is straight and vertical?

Things you will need

- R/C car
- measuring tape
- masking tape
- Phillips screwdriver

How Does Air Drag Affect the Speed of an R/C Car?

At high speeds, drag—or the force of air against a moving body—greatly affects a vehicle's performance. At the end of a race, dragsters use parachutes to increase drag, which helps slow them down. Other racecars use spoilers (automotive wings mounted on the back of cars) to increase downward force on the drive wheels, which increases their traction (friction with the road) at high speeds. Many trucks have spoilers above the cab to minimize the drag of the large boxy trailer behind them. In both cases, spoilers are positioned to deflect air flow.

The force of air resistance increases quickly as the speed of the car increases. Doubling the vehicle's speed increases drag by a factor of 4. The power required to overcome drag at high speeds increases even faster. When the speed doubles, the power used to overcome drag increases by a factor of 8. For a car traveling over 30 miles per hour, wind resistance slows the car more than the friction of the tires on the road.

COOL!

You can measure the effects of air motion and drag on an R/C car. Repeat Experiment 2.2 for measuring the top speed of your car. This time, your car will be slowed down by additional air resistance of plastic produce bags acting like the parachutes behind a drag racer.

1. Use string to tie a lightweight plastic bag to the rear of your car. Tie it at four different points so that it will open and fill with air when the car is moving forward (see Figure 16).

Things you will need

- **R/C car**
- **several plastic produce bags (the kind you get at a grocery store)**
- **string**
- **stopwatch**
- **a friend**
- **measuring tape**
- **masking tape**
- **notebook and pen**

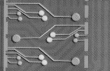

FIGURE 16
Use string to attach a plastic bag to the back of an R/C car. Measure the car's speed with and without the bag in place to gauge the effect of air drag.

2. Use the same test range you used in Experiment 2.2 to measure your car's top speed. Start the car in front of the timing line so that it can reach full speed before you begin timing it. Have a friend measure the time it takes to go from the starting line to the finish line. Repeat this measurement at least three times.

3. Calculate the speed by dividing the length of the test range by the average time it takes the car to complete it.

4. Compare the speed of the car pulling the bag to its speed when it wasn't pulling it.

5. Try other size bags. Repeat the process with larger or smaller plastic bags.

6. Compare the speeds of the car using different size bags. Measure the size of the bags. Fill each with a measurable material. Water would work well. Use a container of known size (for example, a 1-liter water bottle) to fill the bags and record how many bottles of water are required. Compare and graph the volume of the bags to the speed of the car.

Measure Stopping Distance with a Parachute

Skydivers and dragsters both use parachutes to slow them down. How effective would a parachute (bag) be in slowing your R/C car?

1. Repeat Experiment 2.4, which measures the deceleration of the car. This time, measure the stopping distance, too.

2. With a plastic bag tied to the back of your car, measure the time it takes the car to come to a stop. First, mark a starting line with masking tape on the ground. Drive the car along a straight line until it crosses this line. As it crosses, release your grip on the remote-control button.

Things you will need

- R/C car
- stopwatch
- plastic bags
- masking tape
- measuring tape
- string
- a friend to help you measure
- notebook and pen

3. Have a friend start the stopwatch as the car crosses the starting line.

4. Let the car coast to a stop, and then stop the watch. Measure the distance from the starting line to the stopped car. Repeat the experiment at least three times. Did the parachute open each time? If not, repeat the test and use only data obtained when the parachute opened.

5. Calculate an average stopping time and distance. Compare them to the average stopping time and distance without a parachute. How effective is the parachute in slowing down the car? Would two parachutes be twice as effective? Give it a try.

CHAPTER 5

How Much Can Your R/C Car Carry and Pull?

One measure of the power of a vehicle is its capacity to tow objects. In this chapter you can measure how fast your R/C car goes while towing or dragging a rope. Then you can use that information to predict the car's absolute towing capacity.

How Does Dragging a Rope Affect Speed?

For this experiment, use a piece of rope, about 3/16 inch in diameter and about 8 to 10 meters (25 to 30 feet) long. You can use other size ropes. Use enough to make the car slow noticeably. This experiment will tax the batteries, so start with a fresh set or a fresh charge if they are rechargeable.

1. Tie the rope to the back of your car so that it drags freely behind the car. You could loop the middle of the rope through windows in the car or through the rear bumper (see Figure 17).

Things you will need

- R/C car
- rope
- masking tape
- measuring tape
- notebook and pen
- scissors
- stopwatch
- a friend
- notebook and pen

FIGURE 17

By dragging different lengths of rope, you can determine how drag affects speed. Measure both the length of the rope and the speed of the car.

2. Test-drive the car to ensure that the car can pull this length. Do not drive the car with a load it cannot move. Running power through the motor when it cannot turn will quickly ruin the motor. If the car cannot drag the initial length, cut a few feet off the rope and try it again.

3. Set up a test track about 3 meters (10 feet) long. Mark the start and end lines with masking tape. You will want to start the car so that it reaches top speed before it hits the start line.

4. Stream the rope out behind the car in a straight line so that there is no slack. Then, with the help of someone operating a stopwatch, time the car from the moment it crosses the start line to when it crosses the finish line. Calculate the car's speed (distance divided by time) and compare it to the speed you calculated in Experiment 2.2. Would you expect the speed to be much slower when the car is dragging the long rope? Do the measurements prove this?

5. If you have not measured the rope's length accurately, do it now. Measure only the rope that is touching the ground. Any rope supported between the car and the ground shouldn't be measured. Record this length.

6. How many trials do you want to run? You should do at

least ten. Divide the length of rope by the number of trials you want to run. If the initial rope is 10 meters (30 feet) long, and if you want to run the experiment 10 times, you will reduce the length of the rope by 1 meter (3 feet) each trial, because 10/10 = 1.

7. Once you have recorded the data in your notebook, reduce the length of the rope by the length you just calculated. Measure the rope precisely each time you reduce its length. Then time the car again over the test track.

8. Collect all the pairs of data points (length of rope being dragged and the car's speed over the test track) in a data table. Mark the units for both measurements: feet and feet/second or meters and meters/second. Then graph the data. You should be able to look at the graph and quickly understand how rope length affects speed. (A sample graph is shown on page 69.)

9. What story does the graph tell? Do the data points form a regular line? If they do, that suggests that a mathematical relationship exists between the rope length and car speed. Is the line straight? If it is, a change in rope length gives a proportional change in speed. If the line curves, a change in rope length has different impacts on the speed. Study the graph to see what it tells you.

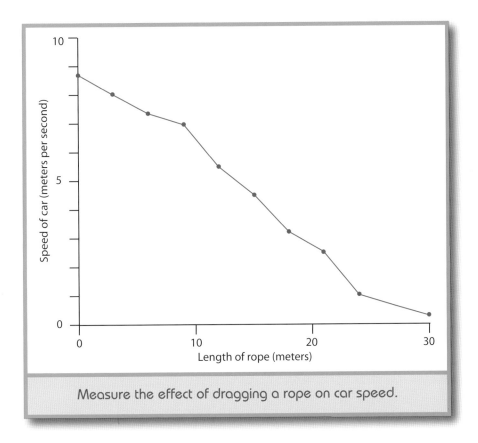

Measure the effect of dragging a rope on car speed.

Record your interpretations of the data and graph in your notebook.

Although you cannot reliably make predictions beyond the data that you collected, you can make projections based on the data. Even if you did not load the car to the point where the motor failed, you can project where that point might be.

Ideally you should repeat the first trial, the one using

the full length of rope, after finishing all the other trials to determine whether loss of battery charge has affected your data. If this final run with the full length of rope has the same speed as the first run, you will know that the batteries did not lose enough charge during the experiment to affect the data. To do this, you will need an identical length of the same rope.

Motors and Turning Power

An electric motor will stall or stop turning when the resistance to turning exceeds its torque, or turning power. Holding the shaft of a running electric motor and stopping it from turning will stall the motor. The motor will draw more current from the battery, and electric resistance will cause its temperature to rise. The heat can quickly damage the motor. Large industrial motors have circuits that cut off the electric power when they sense a stall may occur.

Project the Towing Capacity

If you had run the previous experiment with a rope long enough to stall the car (not a good idea, as you might ruin the motor), you would get a data point along the axis where speed is zero. Since you did not collect this data, you cannot say for certain at what length of rope this would have occurred. However, you can look at the line on your graph and extend it to the rope-length axis. This point is an estimate of the rope length that would have stalled the car.

1. Look at the graph you created in the previous experiment. Notice the shape of the line that connects the data points. Follow the arc of the line with a pencil. Keeping the same shape, pencil in an extension that reaches the length axis.

2. Read the value of the rope length where the line you drew crosses the axis. At this point, the speed is zero.

Things you will need

- data and graph from Experiment 5.1
- notebook and pen

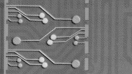

Since a speed of zero indicates a stall, you can project that the maximum towing or dragging capacity is slightly less than the length of rope where the extended line crosses the axis. Record your estimate in your notebook.

Ideas for a Science Fair Project

- How would the towing speed vary with the same length of different materials? Would sisal rope give more drag than nylon?

- Would the speed vary with the size (diameter) of the rope?

Measure the Impact of Dragging Materials

Experiment with other materials towed behind your car.

1. Collect different samples of cloth or carpet squares cut to the same size and shape.

2. Drag each sample behind the car and measure the car speed as outlined in Experiment 5.1.

    What can you infer from your data and observations? How do they compare to your results with the rope?

Things you will need

- R/C car
- stopwatch
- cloth or carpet samples
- notebook and pen
- masking tape
- measuring tape
- a friend

How Increasing the Load Affects Speed

How does weight affect your R/C car's performance? If you add weight to the car, would it travel at a higher speed? Or would it be slower? Would it accelerate faster or slower? In the previous experiments you dragged a rope to see how additional friction impacted the speed of your car. Here, you will add weight but won't increase friction.

Testing your car's performance under different weight conditions is a fun project that could easily become a

Things you will need

- R/C car
- uniform weights—10 or more objects of the same weight, such as bolts or fishing weights
- stopwatch
- plastic container
- tape or string
- track as described in Experiment 2.2
- measuring tape
- a friend
- notebook and pen

science fair project. You can measure the weight you add and measure the change in speed. Then you can graph the numerical data to determine any relationship between the variable (weight) and the result (speed).

Before tying a brick to your car, know that you can damage the motor. Do not continue to hold down the Drive control when the car cannot move. A heavy load can cause the motor to stall and quickly heat up. This heat can damage the motor. Because the extra weight will tax the motor, be sure to start with fresh or recharged batteries.

What can you use for weights, and how do you weigh them? It is easiest to pick objects of a uniform weight. An example might be large nuts or bolts from a hardware store, or lead weights for fishing from a sporting goods store. Having all the objects weigh the same will make it easier to keep track of the load.

Imagine a sports car and a cement truck at a red light. Once the light changes, which one will get through the intersection first? In this experiment, your R/C car's performance will change from mimicking a sports car to a cement truck.

1. Find a container to hold the weights on your car. A plastic container from a grocery store may work.

2. Attach the container to your car so that it won't fall off. Tape or tie it in place.

3. Using a track like the one described in Experiment 2.2, measure your car's top speed with the container in place. Drive the car up to full speed before it crosses the start line. Continue to drive the car in a straight line until it crosses the stop line. Your friend should start the watch when the car crosses the tape marking the start of the test track and stop the watch when it crosses the stop line. Record the data (time) in your notebook.

4. Measure the length of the test track (from the start line to the stop line) and record this distance. Find the speed by dividing the distance of the test track by the time it took the car to travel this distance for each trial. What are the units? Feet per second? Meters per second? If you will use these experiments in a science fair, check what units are required and convert yours if necessary.

5. Add all the weights to the container and measure the car's top speed.

6. If the two speeds are the same or nearly the same, you will need either more weights or heavier weights. If the second speed measurement is significantly slower,

repeat the experiment, removing one weight each time. Record the data.

7. Repeat the experiment with no weights in the container. Is the speed very close to the first measurement? If not, the batteries might be losing their charge.

8. Study your data table showing weight and speed. Do you see a steady change in the speed as the weight changes? Are there one or more speeds that look unusual? Are they too fast or slow compared to the speeds around them? If the data are wildly out of line compared to the others, you should retest that weight or those weights. Ideally you should repeat each part of the experiment three times and average the results.

9. The best way to understand what is happening (and to show other people what is happening) is to graph the data. Make a graph with the car's speed as one axis and the added weight as the other axis. Plot the data. Lightly draw a line to connect each adjacent data point. What does the line look like? Is it straight? Does it curve noticeably upward or downward?

If the line between data points closely resembles a straight line, what does that tell you? What about a curving line?

If each weight you added caused the same change in speed, the line would be straight. Of course, you cannot measure the times exactly, nor can you steer the car exactly the same way for each trial, so expect some variability in the data.

If you cannot draw any line that passes through or near all the data, it suggests that there is great variability in the data. That might be due to problems measuring the time or it could be variability in the car itself. Can you think of a way to find the cause of such variability?

Idea for a Science Fair Project

In Experiment 5.4, you tested the effect of weight on the speed of an R/C car. You could also test the effect of weight on the acceleration of a car.

How Much Weight Can Your Car Pull?

If, instead of carrying weight, the R/C car pulls weight on a sled, what impact does this weight have on speed? Tractor pulls are weight-dragging contests that resemble this experiment.

1. Create a sled using a small piece of cardboard, plastic, or wood. Attach it to your car with a simple harness, such as two paper clips that hook on to the car's rear bumper and are tied to the sled (see Figure 18).

Things you will need

- R/C car
- string
- paper clips
- cardboard, plastic, or wood
- uniform weights—10 or more objects of the same weight, such as bolts or fishing weights, or bottled water
- masking tape
- measuring tape
- stopwatch
- a friend
- notebook and pen

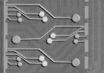

FIGURE 18 You can vary the weight towed behind an R/C car either by adding uniform weights or by adding water to a container.

2. Drive the car with the sled attached to see how the sled tracks behind the car. You want it to closely follow the car's path and to be pulled evenly so that it does not slide from side to side. Then test the sled to see how it holds added weight. Also, get an idea of how much weight the car can tow (maximum towing capacity). Remember not to have the car try to pull a load that is so heavy it cannot move, as this will damage the motor.

3. Set up a test track and mark it with tape. You could use the test track you laid out in Experiment 2.2. Measure the length of the track.

4. Run the first trial with no weights. As your partner controls the car, use a stopwatch to time the car on the track. Then add a few of the weights or a measured amount of water in a water bottle to the sled. Repeat the experiment. Be sure to record the times for each run.

5. Did the car travel much more slowly when dragging the weight? If it did, continue the experiment with less added weight. If it traveled at nearly the same speed as without weight on the sled, add more weight and retest it.

6. Continue adding or removing weights until you have at least 10 trials with different amounts of weight.

7. Graph the data as you did in Experiment 5.4. Be sure to mark the axes showing what they represent and what the units of measurement are. What is the shape of the line connecting the data points? If you were to extend the line beyond the last data point, keeping the same curve, where would this extension cross the zero velocity line? This is the projection, or estimate, of where the car motor would fail.

Look at the line connecting the data points and estimate the maximum safe towing load. This is the type of projection that car and truck manufacturers have to do. They need to tell vehicle owners what loads they can tow without incurring damage.

Idea for a Science Fair Project

A different experiment would be to test how different floor surfaces impact the speed as the car pulls a weighted sled. You might expect that a carpet with deep pile would slow a car much more than a smooth floor would. But can you show that in an experiment? Try many different floor surfaces to find which are the fastest and slowest.

Does Wheel Size Affect Your Car's Performance?

Would your car go faster if it had larger wheels? How could you test the effect of changing the wheel size on the car's performance?

Most inexpensive R/C cars have the wheels glued to the axles. More expensive hobby cars have removable wheels. It can be difficult to remove glued wheels, and even more difficult to get them back on the axles. Instead of removing the wheels, can you figure out another way to make them larger?

How Can You Increase the Size of the Wheels?

1. Locate a pair of wheels or tires that are larger than the ones on your R/C car. Check hobby stores, thrift stores, or science catalogs. An ideal tire would be large enough to fit over your car's current wheels. A good wheel would be slightly larger than the existing wheel. If the wheels you find are much larger than the original wheels, they may not fit under the car body. Rubber bands stretched across the wheels can help hold them in place (see Figure 19).

2. Test the car with the new wheels. If the wheels or tires slip, try accelerating the car from a stop with a series of pulses

Things you will need

- **R/C car**
- **one or more sets of large wheels or tires**
- **masking tape**
- **rubber bands**
- **stopwatch**
- **measuring tape**
- **a friend**
- **notebook and pen**

FIGURE 19

A simple way to increase wheel size is to mount larger wheels over the existing ones.

on the Forward button. Can you control the car with the new wheels or tires? Record what steps you had to take to keep the wheels or tires in place.

Other wheel options to try would be to attach CDs to the wheels or to attach cardboard or wood wheels. A different approach is to build up the diameter of the existing tires by adding layers of masking tape. Even a few wraps can significantly increase the effective wheel/tire size.

Measuring Speed with Larger Drive Wheels

1. If you still have the original test track from Experiment 2.2, use it. Otherwise, make a test track and mark the start

and finish lines with masking tape. Measure the track and record the length.

2. With oversized wheels attached to the car, measure the car's top speed. Start the car far enough before the start line so that it can accelerate to its top speed. Have your friend start the stopwatch when the car crosses the start line and stop it when it crosses the finish line.

3. Record the time and repeat the experiment at least twice. Average the results.

4. Compare this newly measured speed to the original speed measurement from Experiment 2.2. Is the car faster with larger wheels?

5. Increase the wheel size again and measure the speed. Does the car go faster?

Idea for a Science Fair Project

Have you noticed how large racing bike wheels are compared to the wheels on a tricycle? What is the advantage of large wheels? What stops someone from making a bike with really huge wheels? If you can find several sets of wheels with different diameters, you could repeat Experiment 6.1 and graph the results. Graph the wheel diameter versus top speed. What does the data tell you about changing the wheel size?

Increasing the Size of the Front Wheels

COOL!

What happens when you increase the size of both the front and rear wheels? Does increasing the size of both the drive wheels and the turning wheels affect the car's top speed?

1. After you have measured the speed of your car with a pair of oversized wheels on the driving wheels, add a pair of oversized wheels to the front, or non-driving, wheels.

2. Measure the top speed of the car and compare it to the results with oversized wheels on the driving wheels. Does the size of the front wheels change the car's top speed?

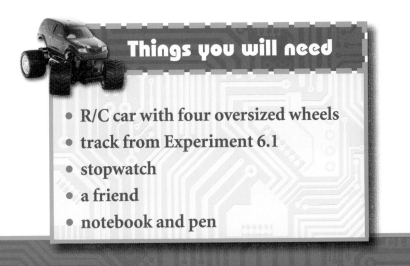

Things you will need

- R/C car with four oversized wheels
- track from Experiment 6.1
- stopwatch
- a friend
- notebook and pen

Make a Radio-Controlled Car

In this chapter, you will learn how to make a model car, convert it into an electric-powered car, and operate it remotely. Finally, you will try converting it to a radio-controlled car. The following experiments guide you in making and testing a series of model cars. Start by making a simple model car without a motor.

Make a Model Car

If you are purchasing wheels for your model, make sure that they will fit onto an axle that you can find (see Figure 20). Many wheels have odd-sized center openings that make them difficult to mount on axles. Common wood dowel sizes are 1/8 inch, 3/16 inch, and 1/4 inch. Small plastic wheels that fit 1/8-inch-diameter wood dowels are recommended. Wheels that fit onto 1/4-inch dowels will work, too.

Things you will need

- **material for the body: cardboard, craft sticks, milk cartons, or other stiff, lightweight materials**
- **scissors**
- **dowels for axles**
- **wheels to fit on dowels**
- **saw for cutting dowels**
- **objects to use as weights, such as bolts or fishing weights**
- **ramp for testing the car, such as a folding table**
- **hot glue or fast-drying glue**
- **masking tape**
- **straws large enough to fit over the dowels**
- **notebook, pen, and marker**

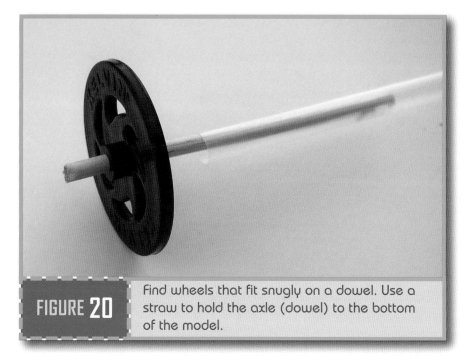

FIGURE 20 | Find wheels that fit snugly on a dowel. Use a straw to hold the axle (dowel) to the bottom of the model.

It is easiest to use wheels that have a center hole that goes completely through the wheel. The axle can then go through the wheel to support the wheel on each side.

Depending on your choice of wheels, you can have an odd number (for example, 3 wheels) or an even number. Besides appearance, is there a reason to choose a particular number of wheels? Each wheel rubs the floor as the car moves, and the friction causes a loss of energy. You might find it easier to align axles that have two wheels apiece. If the axles are not aligned, the car will always turn.

You can find wheels and dowels at science supply stores or in some hobby stores.

1. Cut cardboard or other stiff material into a rectangle about 10 cm (4 in) wide by 20 cm (8 in) long. This will be the body for your car. Other sizes and shapes will work, but you'll want to make your first model a small rectangle.

2. Draw two parallel lines on the underside of the body, one across each end.

3. Glue pieces of straw onto the bottom of the body along the lines you drew.

4. Cut two axles from dowels. The axles should be long enough to extend beyond the ends of the straws and still have enough room for the wheels to fit onto each end.

5. Attach one wheel to each axle. Insert the axles into the straws. Attach a second wheel to each axle. Make sure that the straws do not rub against the wheels. Also, do not bend the straw, which could cause it to rub the axle.

6. Try spinning each set of wheels. Do the wheels turn easily? Do they continue to spin after you release them? If not, find out why the wheels are not turning. It could be that glue is holding the wheel or axle to the bearing, or that the wheel is rubbing against the bearing. If the wheels cannot

spin freely, the car will not move fast with a motor. Find where it is rubbing and make a change to eliminate it.

7. Try rolling the model down an inclined ramp. A large piece of cardboard will do. Or, collapse the legs on one end of a folding table to make a ramp.

8. If the car does not roll in a straight line, realign the axles. If the axles aren't parallel to each other, the car will always turn. It will turn in one direction going forward and the other direction going backward.

9. What happens to the car at the bottom of the ramp? Does it jump? The car loses energy if the car jumps when it hits a bump. See if you can eliminate all design problems that are causing the car to lose energy.

10. How far does the car roll? When the car stops, measure the distance from the bottom of the ramp to the back of the car and record it in your notebook. What changes to the car would make it roll farther? Try one change at a time and test it. Record what change you made and how far the car rolled as a result of that change.

11. Would adding weight help the car travel farther? Tape some weights to the car and retest it. If the car rolls farther with weights, try adding even more weights. Record what weights you used and how far the car rolled.

Make an Electric Car

When you have a model car that rolls far, you can add a motor. Start with the easiest approach: use a propeller.

The motor, alligator clip leads, and propeller are available from science supply stores and from some hobby stores. When purchasing these, make sure that the motor shaft is the same size as the center hole in the propeller. The motor can be an inexpensive toy motor. You can use a 9-volt battery or a battery pack that holds four AA batteries. Although four

Things you will need

- **an adult**
- **model car from Experiment 7.1**
- **small electric motor**
- **2 alligator clip leads**
- **9-volt battery, or a battery pack with 4 AAs**
- **propeller**
- **masking tape**
- **stopwatch**
- **measuring tape**
- **notebook and pen**
- **hot glue (optional)**
- **strip of cardboard (optional)**

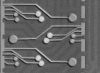

FIGURE 21

Propellers tend to fly off motor shafts unless they are pushed on fully.

FIGURE 22

There are several ways to use an electric motor to propel a model car. In a propeller car, the motor is not attached to the wheels or axles, and the car avoids problems with tire traction.

FIGURE 23

Use alligator clip leads to make connections to motors and batteries or battery cases.

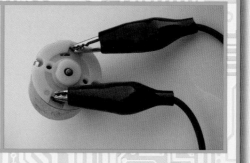

AAs provide less voltage (6 volts) than the 9-volt battery, they will work, and they may be less expensive.

1. **Ask an adult** to push the propeller onto the motor shaft (see Figure 21). The propeller must be pushed on as far as it will go to ensure that it will not fly off.

2. Place the motor with the propeller on the back of the car frame from Experiment 7.1, with the car on a table (see Figure 22). With your other hand, turn the propeller. Do the blades touch the table? If they do, you will need to raise the motor high enough so that the blades will not hit. One way to do this is to glue or tape the motor to the side of the 9-volt battery. A tiny dab of hot glue can hold the motor onto the battery and allow you to remove it later. An alternative is to cut a strip of cardboard and make a stand to hold the motor above the car body.

3. Glue or tape the motor in place. Check to see that the car will not tip over with the weight of the battery and motor. If it does, reposition both toward the center of the car.

4. Connect one end of each of the alligator clip leads to each of the terminals on the electric motor (see Figure 23). The terminals are small metal tabs that stick out on the back of the motor.

5. Connect the free end of one of the clip leads to one of the terminals of the battery. Now you are ready to test your car.

6. Put the car on the floor. Check to see that nothing is in its path. When you complete the electric circuit by connecting the second clip lead to the second battery terminal, the motor will spin very fast. If the propeller hits your finger, it will hurt, so keep your fingers away from it. If you are concerned about your fingers, ask the adult to help. Make the connection and let the car move.

7. Test the car. Make a test track like the one in Experiment 2.2 and measure it. Place the car several feet before the start line of the track. Drive the car across the start and finish lines while the adult times the car. Record the time and the distance. Try this twice more. Record the times and average them. Disconnect one of the two wires from the battery to stop the motor.

Idea for a Science Fair Project

What other ways can you think of to get power from the motor to propel the car? Could you use gears or belts? See Figure 24 for one idea.

motor

belt

FIGURE 24   A student-built electric car uses a rubber band to carry power from the motor to the drive axle.

Reversing the Leads

What would happen if you switch the positions of the two wires (clip leads) on the battery? Let's try it.

1. Disconnect the remaining clip lead from the battery and reconnect it to the other terminal.

2. With the car in position on the floor, connect the second clip lead to the other battery terminal. What happens?

3. Test the speed of the car. Repeat Experiment 7.2 and record the time the car takes to travel between the start and finish lines of the test track. How does this time compare to the previous experiment? Which wiring direction provided faster travel? Why do you think the car went faster one way than the other?

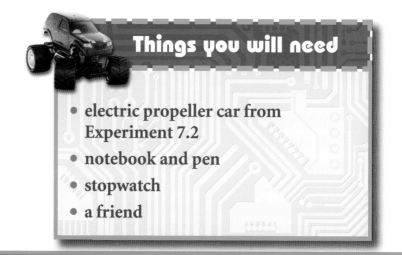

Things you will need

- **electric propeller car from Experiment 7.2**
- **notebook and pen**
- **stopwatch**
- **a friend**

4. Does it matter if you change the leads to the battery or change those going to the motor?

5. When you change leads, what is happening to the direction of the flow of electrons in the wires?

Idea for a Science Fair Project

As a propeller spins, some of the air it pushes escapes over the end of the blades. This escaping air doesn't contribute to the forward motion. To improve the power of a propeller system, engineers surround a propeller with a cylinder called a duct. Try making a duct out of paper, a Styrofoam cup, or other material. Attach it to the motor so that the propeller spins inside the duct. Test it to see if the car moves faster. Try other materials and sizes to see which one works best.

Measuring Voltages

You can purchase an inexpensive voltmeter or multimeter at an electronics store or a science supply store. You may find many uses for this tool.

1. Turn the meter on so it is measuring DC volts (DCV). If there are several settings for DC volts, select the lowest voltage range that includes at least 10 volts. Watch the meter display. It should show either 0 volts or a very small voltage.

2. Touch the metal ends of the two probes of the voltmeter to a 9-volt battery (see Figure 25). What does the meter display? Record the voltage you measure in your notebook. Since you are measuring the voltage in a 9-volt battery, you might expect the display to show 9 volts. But if the battery is new, the voltage will be higher than 9 volts. If it has been used for several experiments, it might be lower. Read the label on the battery. If the battery is an alkaline

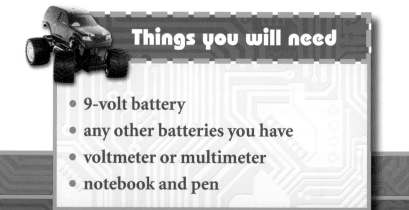

Things you will need

- **9-volt battery**
- **any other batteries you have**
- **voltmeter or multimeter**
- **notebook and pen**

FIGURE 25

Use a voltmeter or multimeter to measure the voltage of a battery or the voltage drop across a motor.

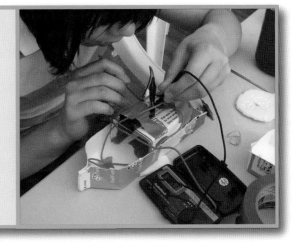

battery (which it most likely is), it will hold its voltage close to 9 volts throughout most of its life.

3. Reverse the two voltmeter leads. That is, take one from the terminal it is on and touch it to the other battery terminal. Switch the position of the second lead to the other side of the battery. What does the meter show now? If your first measurement was a positive number, now you will see a negative number. By switching the leads, you are having electricity flow through the meter in the opposite direction. This will not hurt the meter.

4. Measure the voltage in any other batteries you have. Compare what you measure to the battery rating printed on the side. All of the common cylindrical batteries (AAA, AA, C, and D) are rated at 1.5 volts.

Measuring Voltages While the Motor Is Running

In Experiment 7.4, you measured voltages in a battery that was not connected to a circuit. Now measure the voltage when the battery is powering the motor on your car. Not all voltmeters allow current measurements, so examine the meter you have to see if it does. Look for markings around the dial that show DCA, which stands for *direct current amperes*.

1. Have a friend hold the car and connect the battery to the motor with the two clip leads. The motor can be spinning in either direction (clockwise or counterclockwise).

2. Turn on the meter to DCV and the low range. Touch the probes to the two battery terminals. What voltage do you measure? Record this in your notebook. How does it

Things you will need

- **operating electric motor car (from Experiment 7.2)**
- **voltmeter or multimeter**
- **notebook and pen**
- **a friend**

compare to the measurement when the battery was not connected to the motor?

3. With the motor still running, measure the voltage across the motor. That is, touch one meter probe to one of the motor terminals and the other probe to the other terminal. Record the voltage you measured. Is it the same as you measured across the battery in Step 2?

Measuring the voltage of a battery that does not have a load (is not connected to a circuit) does not tell you much. Even a nearly dead battery will show voltage when it does not have a load. The measurement with the motor running is a more accurate measure of the voltage available. If this measurement is substantially less than 9 volts, the battery is nearly dead. If this is the case, watch the meter. It may show decreasing values while you watch. If it does, disconnect the motor for a minute and reconnect it. The voltage will jump up with the motor disconnected and drop down once it is reconnected. During that one-minute interval, the voltage will have risen. It will quickly drop down to the values you measured before.

Measuring Current

Not all voltmeters allow current measurements, so examine the meter you have to see if it does. Look for markings around the dial that show DCA, which stands for *direct current amperes*. If your meter has this, look at the ranges available to use. You will need to measure currents up to a few amps, so look for a scale that goes up to 10 A.

Also look to see where the voltmeter leads should be connected to measure currents. You might have to plug the red lead to a different connector. The connector will be marked on the face of the meter.

1. With the voltmeter cables in the correct connectors, use one clip lead to connect one of the meter probes to one battery terminal. Attach another clip lead from the voltmeter to one of the motor terminals. Use a third clip lead

Things you will need

- **electric motor car you have built**
- **voltmeter that measures electric current**
- **3 alligator clip leads**

to complete the circuit by connecting the open terminal on the battery to the remaining terminal on the motor. Now the meter is in series with the motor.

2. Turn the meter on and switch the dial to measure DCA. Measure and record how much current (measured in amperes) is flowing.

When you measured voltage in Experiment 7.5, you connected the meter probes in parallel to the terminals of either the battery or motor. This allowed you to measure the voltage drop across the terminals. To measure current, the current has to flow through the meter. By measuring both the voltage and current in the circuit, you can calculate how much electrical power the motor is using and then estimate how long the battery will last.

How Much Power Does Your Model Use?

Power is related to how fast energy is flowing. Your electric car uses electric energy to drive the motor. The more power that the battery provides and the motor uses, the faster the car will go. In an electric circuit, power can be calculated by multiplying the voltage by the current.

Multiply the voltage you recorded when the motor was spinning times the current in the circuit. The product of these two measurements is power in units of watts. For example, if you measured a voltage of 3.0 volts (the battery is nearly dead) and a current of 1.4 amperes, the power in the circuit would be 4.2 watts:

$$\text{Power} = 3.0 \times 1.4 = 4.2 \text{ watts}$$

Cool Technology Fact

How does the power of your model car compare to the power produced by an automobile? Check the owner's manual for your family car, or go online to find the power (given as horsepower) for your car. Then convert the power estimate for your model from watts to horsepower.

1 watt = 0.00134 horsepower

Multiply the calculated power in watts by 0.00134 to get the power in horsepower. In the example above, the model car was using power at the rate of 4.2 watts. Converted into units of horsepower, the model was using 0.0056 horsepower. Typical horsepower for a car is 200 to 300. A car weighs 2,000 to 4,000 times as much as the model car, and has many times the power available to move it.

How Long Will Your Battery Last?

COOL!

Batteries are rated by the amount of current they provide for a period of time. This "power rating" is given in amp hours. A battery supplying 1 amp hour would deliver 1 amp for an hour before being exhausted. Or it could deliver 0.5 amp for 2 hours, or any other combination of current and time that equals 1 amp hour.

1. Estimate how long your battery will last. A 9-volt battery can deliver 625 milliamp hours (0.625 amp-hours). Dividing this value by the rate that current flows in the circuit (which you measured) will give the length of the life of the battery. In the example for Experiment 7.6, the current measured was 1.4 amperes, so the life of the battery is 27 minutes (0.625 amp-hours/1.4 amps = 0.45 hr x 60 min = 27 min). So this model can get approximately 27 minutes of life from a 9-volt battery.

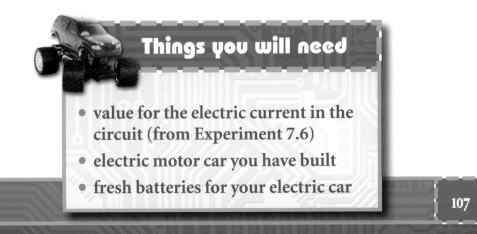

Things you will need

- **value for the electric current in the circuit (from Experiment 7.6)**
- **electric motor car you have built**
- **fresh batteries for your electric car**

2. Calculate the life of the battery you are using and record it. Use the table below to find the power rating of the batteries you are using. Using fresh batteries, keep track of the time your model runs and see if the life of the battery matches what you have calculated. Note that most R/C cars use multiple batteries connected in series so they are acting as a single battery with multiple cells.

Battery type	Power rating (milliamp hours)
9 volt	625
AAA	1,250
AA	2,850
C	8,350
D	20,500

Make a Direct Drive Car

There are other designs to try for powering a model car with an electric motor. One is direct drive, in which a wheel is mounted directly on the motor shaft. Most wheels have center openings larger than the motor shaft, so you will have to engineer a way to keep the wheel on the shaft (see Figure 26).

1. Remove the electric motor from your electric motor car and take off the propeller. **You may need adult help** to get the propeller off.

2. Take a wheel off one of the axles and slide it onto the motor shaft. Does it fit? If the motor shaft is smaller than the hole in the wheel, try hot-gluing the wheel onto the shaft. Be careful not to get hot glue on your fingers. An alternative is to build up the size of the motor shaft with

Things you will need

- **an adult**
- **electric motor car you have built**
- **hot glue or tape**
- **drill (optional)**
- **stopwatch**

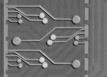
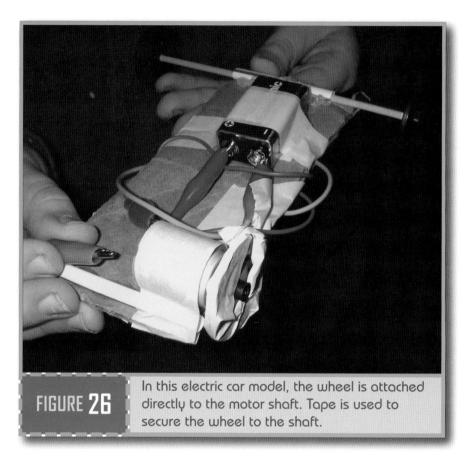

FIGURE 26 In this electric car model, the wheel is attached directly to the motor shaft. Tape is used to secure the wheel to the shaft.

small pieces of tape. Wrap the tape around the shaft until it just barely squeezes into the wheel opening.

3. If the motor shaft is too large to fit into the wheel, **ask an adult** to drill out the hole in the wheel so it will fit.

4. When the wheel is firmly on the motor shaft, decide where on the model you will locate this drive wheel. Will you make a 3-wheel car with the drive motor at one end

and two other wheels on an axle at the other end? Or do you have another design in mind?

5. Finish the model and connect the motor to the battery. Test the car by measuring the time it takes to cross a test track, such as the one you made in Experiment 2.2. How does this compare to the propeller car? Which is faster?

Unlike the previous model where wheel traction with the ground was not a problem, here it will be an issue. After you build and test the model, watch the drive wheel to see how much it is slipping as it spins. How can you increase the traction or decrease the slippage?

Options include decreasing the battery voltage by using one to four AA batteries instead of a 9-volt. A lower voltage power supply will produce lower current, and turn the motor more slowly, which will result in less slippage. Increasing the weight directly above the drive wheel or adding higher-friction material to the wheel rim are other possible olutions.

Make a Belt-Drive Car

One more option is to drive the car with a belt or rubber band (see Figure 27). A rubber band carries the energy generated by the motor to the axle. Pulleys on both the driveshaft and the axle help hold the rubber band, but the model can work without them. The rubber band can go directly onto the motor shaft and axle without pulleys, but this arrangement requires angling the motor shaft away from the axle so the rubber band does not slide off the shaft. Science supply stores sell pulleys.

1. Remove the wheel from the motor shaft of your electric motor car.

Things you will need

- electric motor car you have built
- rubber bands
- pulleys that fit onto the motor shaft and onto an axle (optional)
- a friend
- glue
- stopwatch

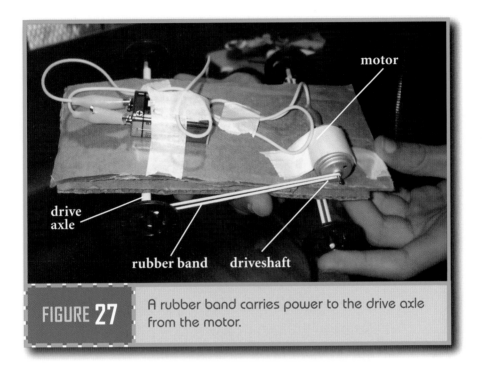

motor

drive axle

rubber band   driveshaft

FIGURE 27   A rubber band carries power to the drive axle from the motor.

2. If you have pulleys, slide one onto one of the axles. You will need to remove one wheel, slide the pulley on, and then replace the wheel. Put another pulley on the driveshaft.

3. Loop a rubber band onto the axle (or the pulley that is on the axle) and onto the driveshaft. Stretch the rubber band to determine how far away from the axle the motor should be located. The tension in the belt should not be so tight that the motor cannot turn or the axle bends under the strain; it also should not be so loose that it slips as the motor turns. To keep the belt from sliding off the

shaft, you either have to angle the motor so that the shaft is pointing slightly away from the axle it is connected to, or you have to put something on the end of the shaft to keep the belt in place.

4. Mark the location of the motor on the car body. Remove the rubber band and glue the motor to the car body.

5. Try the belt-drive system while holding the car in the air. Does the belt stay on the motor shaft? If not, pull the motor off the body and glue it in a new position where the rubber band will stay on.

6. Test the car and measure its speed. Have a friend operate the stopwatch while you run the car over a test track, such as the one you made in Experiment 2.2. Which of the three drive mechanisms (propeller, direct drive, or belt drive) gives the fastest speed?

These cars are great fun, part of which is chasing after them as they zoom across the floor. But if you want to be able to control their motion, you have to add either a wire remote control or radio remote control. Let's convert your model into a remote-controlled car.

Make a Remote-Controlled Car

Electronics stores carry wire, switches, and wire strippers. The switch can be a momentary contact switch, which is a switch that turns the circuit on only when the switch is depressed, or it could be a throw switch, which has a lever that can be moved to the off or on position. See what type of switch you can find.

1. Cut two pieces of 18- or 20-gauge wire, each about 3 meters (9 feet) long.

2. Use the strippers to remove about 1 cm (½ in) of insulation from both ends of both wires. If you do not have wire strippers, you can hold the end of the wire in a pair of scissors.

Things you will need

- **an adult**
- **electric motor car you have built**
- **roll of electric wire (18- to 20-gauge)**
- **wire stripper or scissors**
- **small electric switch**
- **alligator clip leads**
- **soldering gun**
- **stopwatch**

Cut the insulation with the scissors, without cutting through the metal wire, and then pull the wire through the scissors to remove the insulation.

3. Connect one end of one wire to one of the motor terminals. You can use an alligator clip lead to make the connection to the terminal.

4. Connect one end of the other wire to one of the battery terminals using an alligator clip lead.

5. Use a clip lead to connect the other motor terminal to the other battery terminal.

6. Test your wiring. Touch the distant ends of the two wires to see if the motor spins and the car moves. If it does, you have made a remote control for your car.

7. Connect the two ends of the two wires to the terminals of a switch. Use alligator clip leads to make temporary connections. When you are sure the circuit is working with the switch, move the clip leads and **have an adult** solder the wires to the switch.

8. Test your car to see if its speed has changed. Have the adult time the car as you drive it over the start and finish lines of a test track. Compare the speed of the remote-controlled car to its speed without the remote control.

Convert Your Remote-Controlled Car to a Radio-Controlled Car

This experiment helps you use the radio-controlled circuits in an old R/C car in the electric car that you have built. You can get old R/C cars at garage sales and thrift stores. Even if the car does not work, its circuits may work when you use them in the car you have built. Be sure to get both the R/C car and the handheld controller that goes with it. Check on the back of the controller and the bottom of the car to see that both operate at the same frequency.

1. Use the screwdriver to remove the car body from its frame. Beneath the body you will find the circuit board

Things you will need

- old R/C car that you have taken apart
- electric motor car you have built
- Phillips screwdriver
- flat-head screwdriver
- masking tape
- pen
- wire strippers or scissors
- alligator clip leads

that receives radio signals from the controller and turns the two motors on and off.

2. Find the drive motor, most likely located by the left rear wheel. Follow the wires that power the motor back to the circuit board or battery pack. Label the wires with a piece of masking tape and mark them "motor." You will want to connect the drive motor in your model the same way that the drive motor in the remote-controlled car is connected.

3. Follow the wires that connect the battery case to the circuit board. The battery case is usually housed underneath the car. Most models have a 9-volt battery that powers the circuit board and a separate battery case (usually a bank of AA or C batteries) that powers the motors. Label the wires that provide power and indicate which type of battery and whether the wire is carrying electricity from the + or – side of the battery. The batteries show a small + and –, so you'll know which side is which.

4. Several other wires or connectors come from the circuit board. These include the antenna, the steering motor wires, and any lights. Label these as well.

5. Now cut the wires with scissors or wire strippers, leaving as much wire as possible, with their labels, connected to the circuit board.

6. Remove the circuit board. It may be held in place by some screws or by plastic fasteners. Use a screwdriver to pry the plastic connectors off.

7. Strip the ends of the wires that will conduct electric power to the motor in the car model you made. Use alligator clip leads to connect the motor terminals to the circuit board wires. Use other clip leads to connect the circuit board to batteries, making sure that you are connecting the board in the same way it was connected in the R/C car.

8. Turn on the hand controller and test your model. Does it work? If not, recheck the electrical connections.

9. Try the steering controls. Connect a small motor to the steering wires from the circuit board with alligator clip leads. Does this motor spin when you push the steering control? If it does, what could you do with this control? You could add lights or, with a good design, even steering to your new car.

To add lights, collect individual lights from a strand of holiday lights or get a light fixture from an electronics store.

You want lights that will operate with voltage that is supplied by the battery pack in the car.

Look at how the steering works in the R/C car. That would be difficult to reproduce unless you can cut out the entire front half of the R/C car and add it to the model you made. You could also try duplicating the parts by cutting them out of stiff cardboard with scissors. See if you can figure out any easier ways to get your model to steer.

If you are unable to get the radio controls to work, try the circuit board from another old R/C car. Make sure you label the connections before you cut the wires in the old car and make the same connections to the motor in the model you made. With some persistence you will get your own R/C car to operate.

Glossary

ampere—A measurement of electrical current. One amp of current is the movement of a fixed number (6.24 x 1018) of electric charges in one second.

antenna—A device that converts electrical signals into electromagnetic signals or electromagnetic signals into electrical signals.

brushes—In a motor, the brushes carry electricity from a stationary contact to the moving component of the motor by rubbing against it.

commutator—An electric switch inside a motor that controls the flow of electricity to the rotor.

current—The movement of electric charges. It is measured in amps or amperes.

drag—A force that reduces the speed of motion.

electric circuit—A closed loop of electrical conductors that allows current to travel through the components and back to the power source.

frequency—The number of times a wave crest passes a point in one second.

power—Electric power is rate at which electric energy is used. It is defined to be the voltage multiplied by the current. It is measured in watts.

radio control—In radio control, radio waves are used to control a device at a distance.

remote control—A device that allows a person to control a device at a distance.

torque—The turning force of an engine or other power source as measured from the center of rotation.

voltage—The potential electric energy of a source.

Further Reading

Bartholomew, Alan. *Electric Mischief: Battery-Powered Gadgets Kids Can Build.* Toronto : Kids Can Press, 2002.

Downie, Neil A. *Ink Sandwiches, Electric Worms, and 37 Other Experiments for Saturday Science.* Baltimore: Johns Hopkins University Press, 2003.

Dreier, David. *Electrical Circuits: Harnessing Electricity.* Minneapolis: Compass Point Books, 2008.

Gardner, Robert. *Easy Genius Science Projects With Electricity and Magnetism: Great Experiments and Ideas.* Berkeley Heights, N.J.: Enslow Publishers, Inc., 2009.

Hammond, Richard. *Car Science: An Under-the-Hood, Behind-the-Dash Look at How Cars Work.* London: Dorling Kindersley, 2008.

Pinchuk, Amy. *Make Cool Gadgets for Your Room.* Toronto: Maple Tree Press, 2004.

Internet Addresses

Kenneth Lafferty Hess Family Charitable Foundation. *Science Buddies*. "Free Science Fair Project Ideas, Answers, and Tool for Serious Students." © 2002–2009.
<http://www.sciencebuddies.org >

Science Hound. "All Science Fair Projects." 2008.
<http://www.all-science-fair-projects.com/>

Science Supply Companies

American Science & Surplus

P.O. Box 1030

Skokie, IL 60076

888-724-7587

<http://www.sciplus.com>

KELVIN

280 Adams Blvd.

Farmingdale, NY 11735

800-535-8469

<http://www.kelvin.com>

Index